WHAT IT MEANS TO BE
SERIES

PUBLISHER	Joseph R. DeVarennes
PUBLICATION DIRECTOR	Kenneth H. Pearson
ADVISORS	Roger Aubin
	Robert Furlonger
EDITORIAL MANAGER	Jocelyn Smyth
EDITORS	Ann Martin
	Shelley McGuinness
	Robin Rivers
	Mayta Tannenbaum
ARTISTS	Summer Morse
	Barbara Pileggi
	Steve Pileggi
	Mike Stearns
PRODUCTION MANAGER	Ernest Homewood
PRODUCTION ASSISTANTS	Catherine Gordon
	Kathy Kishimoto
PUBLICATION ADMINISTRATOR	Anna Good

Canadian Cataloguing in Publication Data

Prasad, Nancy
  What it means to be—a good sport

(What it means to be; 19)
ISBN 0-7172-2245-4

1. Sportsmanship — Juvenile literature.
I. Pileggi, Steve.   II. Title.   III. Title: A good sport.   IV. Series.

GV706.3.P73 1987   j175   C87-095062-2

WHAT IT MEANS TO BE...
A GOOD SPORT

Written by
Nancy Prasad

Illustrated by
Steve Pileggi

A good sport plays by the rules.

It was a rainy day and Jason invited some friends over to play cards. They were playing fish. Everyone was laughing and having a good time except for Bobby. He was upset because he hadn't won yet. He didn't like losing very much.

"I don't like this card," complained Bobby as he picked up one from the pile. "I want a different one." And he reached for the pile of cards.

"Stop!" cried Kim. "You can't start changing the rules just to suit yourself."

"That's right," agreed Jason. "If you won't follow the rules, you can't play the game."

"Aaaw," said Bobby. Then he thought about it. He did want to stay. "I'll play by the rules." By the time they stopped playing, he had won three times.

All games and activities have special instructions and rules. If you are a good sport you always follow the rules, and people will like to play with you.

Good sports are willing to try something new.

On Saturday, Hannah and Janice went with their mothers to a nearby shopping mall. They had their hair cut, bought some clothes and tried on lots of shoes.

"Now, can we go to the toy store?" asked Hannah.

Hannah's mom looked at Janice's mom. "Why not?" she said. "We've gone everywhere else."

Inside the toy store they saw a sign saying: Be a Clown For a Day! Beneath it was a clown with brushes and tubes of paint who was painting funny faces on children.

"Oh!" cried Hannah. "That looks like fun. I've always wanted to be a clown. Can we get our faces painted?"

Their mothers agreed and Hannah pulled Janice over to the line-up.

Hannah was bubbling with excitement. "Just two more people, then it's our turn."

Janice looked unhappy. "I don't want to look funny and have people laughing at me."

"But I wanted us to be clowns together," said Hannah. "One clown is a lonely clown." She made such a sad face that Janice had to laugh.

"Next," called the clown.

"That's me!" cried Hannah.

Janice watched the clown paint Hannah's face white and then add a big red mouth, black pointed eyebrows and a red flower on her cheek.

"Maybe I'll give it a try," Janice thought. Before she knew it, she was having her face painted too. "Could I have a butterfly on my cheek?" she asked shyly.

When they were finished, the girls looked at each other and giggled. "This is fun!" exclaimed Janice.

"All we need are big, floppy feet," said Hannah.

Your friends may want to try something and you may be nervous. You can be a good sport by giving it a shot.

Being a good sport means being a good winner and loser.

One day Joey's father brought home a table tennis set and put it up in the basement. "Come on, Joey," he said. "I'll teach you how to play."

Joey played with his father every night for a week. Then he brought some of his friends to show them the new game. Soon Bobby, Paul, Jason and Dylan had all learned the rules.

"Let's have a tournament to see who will be the grand champion," suggested Joey.

"You'll probably win," grumbled Paul. "You've had the most practice."

"No, I'll be the scorekeeper," said Joey. He wrote their names on a big piece of paper and stuck it up on the wall. "We can start tomorrow after school."

By the end of the week everybody had won one game, but Jason and Dylan had each won two games.

"We have to find the grand champion," said Joey. "On Sunday, we'll have the final match between Dylan and Jason."

On Sunday, they all crowded around to watch Jason and Dylan play. It was a long game. They were both very good. Finally, Dylan won.

"Wow!" exclaimed Dylan. "That was hard work! You're really a good player, Jason."

Jason smiled and shook Dylan's hand. "Thanks, Dylan," he said. "That means a lot, coming from the grand champion of table tennis!"

If you lose a game, you should congratulate the winner. When you win, try to say something kind to the loser. That way everyone feels good.

Good sports can laugh at themselves.

Janice loved windy days. She enjoyed watching the trees bending and feeling the wind on her face. She decided to make a kite in kindergarten. It would be the perfect toy for windy days.

For almost a whole week, Janice spent all her free time in class building her kite and decorating it. She was very pleased with her efforts. The kite was bright and colorful and strong. She could hardly wait to show her parents and brother. They would be so surprised and proud of her. Maybe she would make each of them a kite for their birthdays. She might even become a professional kite maker someday. Her daydreams grew and grew.

At last Janice's kite was finished. She put it in a bag to take it home. She didn't want anyone to see it until the right moment.

"Hey, where's the great kite you've been talking about?" asked Jason when she walked in the door.

"You can see it tomorrow morning at 9:30," she said mysteriously.

The next morning Janice was excited. Her kite would fly today! When she walked into the backyard, she was pleased to feel a brisk wind. Her family gathered around to watch her take the kite out of the bag.

"It's nifty," said her dad.

She put it on the grass and unwound some string. "Okay, Jason, throw it into the air."

He threw the kite up and it sank right back to the ground. He tried again and it sank again.

"I don't understand," Janice cried. "Why isn't it flying?"

Her mother examined the kite and started to laugh softly. Then her father and brother joined in. Janice looked from one to the other.

"It's all those beads and pebbles you decorated it with," spluttered Jason.

Then Janice realized: her kite was very beautiful but very heavy. She started to chuckle. "Oh, well, I can always hang it on my wall."

Sometimes things may not go as you expected. Learning to laugh at your mistakes shows you're a good sport.

Good sports look on the positive side of things.

Eva went to the hospital to have her tonsils taken out. When she was back home again, Kim packed her school bag with things she thought Eva might like and started off to visit her. Halfway down the street, Kim met Colette, carrying a bunch of flowers. They were both going to see Eva!

"Poor Eva," said Colette. "I'm going to cheer her up. She must feel sad. Think of all the fun she's missing."

"She must feel lonely too," added Kim as she knocked on Eva's door.

Eva's father let them in and they tiptoed up to Eva's room. Eva smiled at her friends. "Can't talk much," she whispered. "It hurts my throat."

"Don't try to talk, Eva," said Colette. "Just look at what we brought for you." Colette gave Eva some comic books and her schoolwork as well as the flowers from her garden.

Kim gave Eva a book of jokes and riddles, and a diary. "This is a private diary," she explained. "Here's the key. It's for writing about your thoughts and feelings, and anything else you want to remember."

Eva smiled her thanks. The girls told her all their news and looked at her get-well cards. Then they hugged her and left.

Eva picked up her diary and started writing.

Dear Diary, The doctor took my tonsils out. My throat hurts and I can't go out to play. But I am happy. I have my best friends, Kim and Colette. And now I have you too, Dear Diary. It is not so bad being sick with all these good things.

Part of being a good sport is being cheerful when you are sick or unable to do everything you want to do. Remember that there are many good things to be happy about in your life. How many can you think of right now?

Being a good sport means sharing in friends' successes.

Tammy and Hannah were sitting at Tammy's kitchen table drawing and coloring.

"Hey, you two," called Tammy's dad. "Here's something that should interest you."

"What?"

"The shopping center is running an art contest for kids. Why don't you both send a drawing?"

"Yeah!" cried Hannah.

"We might even win," said Tammy.

"We might become famous," exclaimed Hannah.

The two girls laughed and worked on their drawings until they each had one they thought was good. Tammy's dad put the artwork in a big envelope and wrote the address on it. As they mailed it at the corner, Hannah and Tammy each gave it a kiss for good luck.

Two weeks later Tammy received a notice in the mail. She had won second prize for her drawing. She phoned Hannah right away.

"Guess what?" cried Tammy. "I won pencil crayons and special colored paper for getting second place in the art contest."

"Oh," replied Hannah. She was disappointed that she hadn't won.

"They've put my drawing on display in the mall," said Tammy.

"Lucky for you," mumbled Hannah.

"Do you want to come with me to collect my prize and see my drawing? Then we can use my new supplies."

"I guess so," Hannah answered. She was feeling a bit jealous.

But when Hannah saw how happy Tammy was and how eager she was to share her prize, she started to feel proud of her friend. "I'm really glad you did so well, Tammy," she said—and meant it.

When your friends do well at something, you should be happy for them.

If you are a good sport, you are willing to change your plans when things go wrong.

One Friday night Joey arrived at Ryan's house with food, a flashlight and a sleeping bag. He and Ryan were camping out in the backyard.

"First, we'll put up the tent," explained Ryan. "Cameron said he'd help us."

When the tent was up, the boys put their belongings inside.

"How about a marshmallow roast?" asked Ryan's mom.

She made a small fire in the barbecue while the boys got marshmallows and sticks ready. After eating marshmallows and apples, it was time for bed. Ryan's dog Red came to sleep in the tent too.

"This sure is cosy," sighed Joey, snuggling into his sleeping bag.

They soon drifted off to sleep, dreaming of woods, streams and mountains.

Joey dreamed he was swimming in a lake, and the water got colder and colder. He woke up in a puddle of water. Thunder was booming, lightning was flashing and Red was howling.

"Uh-oh," cried Joey and turned on his flashlight. Ryan woke up too. They gazed at the rain trickling in through the torn canvas of the tent.

"This would have to happen," moaned Joey. "It was my first camp out too."

"I have a plan," said Ryan. "Grab your things and follow me." Two wet boys and one wet dog ran into the house. Everyone inside was awake too.

"Mom, do you think we could . . ." Ryan whispered in her ear.

His mother took one look at their disappointed faces. "Sure, you can," she said. And after some milk and cookies, the boys settled down to sleep under a tent of bed sheets in the recreation room.

Unexpected things sometimes happen that may seem to ruin your plans. Be a good sport and use your imagination to find something else you can do and enjoy.

Good sports understand that they cannot always have everything their way.

"Why don't we go out for dinner and a movie on Friday?" suggested Dylan's father.

"That sounds great!" exclaimed Dylan.

"You can bring a friend if you want."

The next day Dylan walked to school with Bobby and invited him. Bobby was delighted to go along.

"Where shall we go to eat?" asked Dylan's father on Friday night.

"Let's go for pizza," suggested Dylan.

"Great!" said Bobby. "We can have one with lots of pineapple."

"And bacon," added Dylan.

"What about anchovies?" asked his dad.

Both boys made faces and shook their heads.

They had dinner at a big old restaurant with an open kitchen. They could see the cooks tossing the pizza dough in the air and catching it. They kept waiting for one to land on someone's head, but none did.

After dinner they walked to the movie theater. There was a long, long line in front of it. When they reached the ticket counter, they found that the comedy they wanted to see was sold out.

"Let's see the wilderness film at the other theater," said Dylan. "It looks exciting."

"That sounds good to me," answered his father. "What do you say, Bobby?"

Bobby wasn't interested in that movie, but since the others wanted to see it, he agreed.

Bobby soon found himself caught up in the story of the kayaker who traveled through the northern forests. He was glad he had seen the movie.

"Maybe next week we can see the comedy," suggested Dylan after the film finished.

"And have anchovies?"

"No way!" cried the two boys.

If you are a good sport you don't have to have your own way all the time. A good sport is flexible and open-minded and willing to accept a friend's decision.

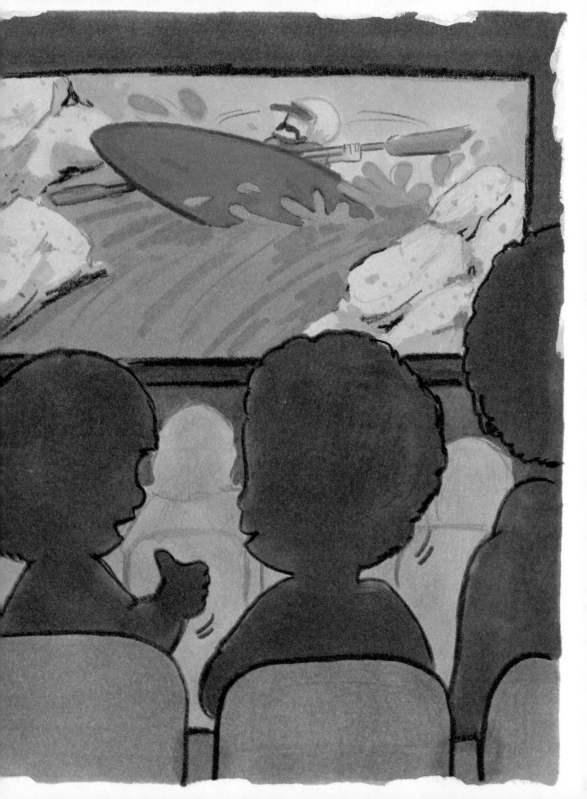

Everyone likes a good sport.

Mr. Corban was sitting on his front porch reading a newspaper when Hannah, Tammy and Mitchell came walking by.

"Whew!" sighed Tammy. "It's so hot today. I wish we could play in my wading pool. Too bad it has a leak."

"My mom is getting me a pool on Saturday," said Hannah. "But that doesn't help us right now."

"I think I'm going to melt," moaned Mitchell.

Mr. Corban called out to them. "You can cool off right away. I'm just about to water my lawn. You can run under the sprinkler."

"Oh, boy!" cried Mitchell. "Let's go put on our bathing suits."

When they got back, the sprinkler was on full force. "Whee!" squealed Hannah as she ran under the shower of water.

"Wait for us!" cried Mitchell and Tammy, running to join her.

The three friends laughed and leaped through the sparkling drops of water. The coolness was marvelous, and suddenly the hot sun started to feel good too.

"Come and try it!" Tammy called to Mr. Corban. "It's so-o-o-o cool!"

Mr. Corban watched for a while, then he went in the house. A few minutes later, he came out wearing his bathing suit. He put a deck chair at the edge of the lawn and sat down. As the sprinkler moved back and forth the water trickled onto him.

"It sure feels good," he said smiling.

Being a good sport means finding ways to help others have a good time—and joining in. You can be a good sport no matter what age you are.

Show younger children how to be good sports by being a good example.

It was a sunny day and Kim and Colette were going berry picking with Colette's mom. "Can Mitch and me go with you?" asked Tammy. "We want to pick berries too."

"It's all right with me," said Kim.

"Me too," added Colette. "But we're staying until we fill four baskets with berries. Mom will make us blueberry pie if we do."

"Yum!" exclaimed Tammy and Mitchell.

They followed the road behind Mr. Martin's house that led to some woods and fields.

"Mr. Martin told me he used to go berry picking here when he was a kid," said Colette.

"And so did I," added her mother.

Mitchell looked around the shadowy woods. "I hope there aren't any bears around here." The older girls laughed.

Tammy looked scared. "There aren't any bears this close to where people live," explained Kim. "I see some berries. Let's start picking."

They started picking close to one another, but soon spread out as they saw bigger and better blueberries. Tammy's basket was almost full when she heard a growling noise in the bushes.

"Oh! A bear!" she yelped, and started running.

She bumped into Colette and their baskets fell, spilling berries all over the ground.

Their mother came running over. "Are you okay?" she asked.

"I thought I heard a bear," cried Tammy.

Tammy picked up her basket. There were only a few berries left in the bottom. "It was such hard work picking these berries," she sobbed. "I don't feel like starting again."

"I don't feel like it either," said Colette. "But I do feel like eating blueberry pie. Come on, I'll help you."

Pretty soon, Mitchell and Kim came along. Their baskets were full. Kim was laughing as Mitchell growled at her. When Tammy heard him she said, "Oh, Mitch. I thought you were a bear, and I ran and spilled my berry basket."

"Sorry," he apologized.

"We'll be glad to help you," said Kim.

Mitchell was about to say, "Do I have to?" when he saw that Kim was already putting berries in Colette's basket. He picked some berries and put them in Tammy's basket. Tammy smiled at him.

Kim and Mitchell stayed for supper at Tammy's house and they had blueberry pie for dessert. "That sure was good," said Mitchell.

Tammy laughed. "Your teeth are blue!"

"So is my tongue," he said, sticking it out.

"I'm glad we stayed to pick extra berries after I dropped my basket," said Tammy. "But the best part was that you all helped me."

And she smiled a big, blueberry smile.

Younger children often want to give up when they run into difficulties. You can show them how to be a good sport by helping and encouraging them. People who are good sports are more fun to live, work and play with. Here are some ways you can be a good sport:
- Try new things with your friends.
- Be willing to laugh at yourself.
- Play by the rules.
- Be a good winner and loser.

Printed and bound in U.S.